The House of Life

Dante Gabriel Rossetti

Contents

PART I. YOUTH AND CHANGE 7
INTRODUCTORY SONNET 7
LOVE ENTHRONED 8
BRIDAL BIRTH 8
REDEMPTION 9
LOVESIGHT 10
HEART'S HOPE 10
THE KISS 11
NUPTIAL SLEEP 12
SUPREME SURRENDER 12
LOVE'S LOVERS 13
PASSION AND WORSHIP 14
THE PORTRAIT 14
THE LOVE-LETTER 15
THE LOVERS' WALK 16
ANTIPHONY 16
YOUTH'S SPRING-TRIBUTE 17
THE BIRTH-BOND 18
A DAY OF LOVE 18
BEAUTY'S PAGEANT 19
GENIUS IN BEAUTY 20
SILENT NOON 20
GRACIOUS MOONLIGHT 21
LOVE-SWEETNESS 22
HEART'S HAVEN 22
LOVE'S BAUBLES 23
PRIDE OF YOUTH 24
WINGED HOURS 24
MID – RAPTURE 25
HEART'S COMPASS 26
SOUL-LIGHT 26
THE MOONSTAR 27
LAST FIRE 28

HER GIFTS	28
EQUAL TROTH	29
VENUS VICTRIX	30
THE DARK GLASS	30
THE LAMP'S SHRINE	31
LIFE – IN – LOVE	32
THE LOVE – MOON	32
THE MORROW'S MESSAGE	33
SLEEPLESS DREAMS	34
SEVERED SELVES	34
THROUGH DEATH TO LOVE	35
HOPE OVERTAKEN	36
LOVE AND HOPE	36
CLOUD AND WIND	37
SECRET PARTING	38
PARTED LOVE	38
BROKEN MUSIC	39
DEATH-IN-LOVE	40
WILLOWWOOD	40
WITHOUT HER	43
LOVE'S FATALITY	44
STILLBORN LOVE	44
TRUE WOMAN	45
LOVE'S LAST GIFT	47

PART II. CHANGE AND FATE 48

TRANSFIGURED LIFE	48
THE SONG-THROE	49
THE SOUL'S SPHERE	49
INCLUSIVENESS	50
ARDOUR AND MEMORY	51
KNOWN IN VAIN	51
HEART OF THE NIGHT	52
THE LANDMARK	53
A DARK DAY	53
AUTUMN IDLENESS	54

THE HILL SUMMIT	55
THE CHOICE	55
OLD AND NEW ART	57
SOUL'S BEAUTY	59
BODY'S BEAUTY	60
THE MONOCHORD	60
FROM DAWN TO NOON	61
MEMORIAL THRESHOLDS	62
HOARDED JOY	62
BARREN SPRING	63
FAREWELL TO THE GLEN	64
VAIN VIRTUES	64
LOST DAYS	65
DEATH'S SONGSTERS	66
HERO'S LAMP	66
THE TREES OF THE GARDEN	67
RETRO ME, SATHANA!'	68
LOST ON BOTH SIDES	68
THE SUN'S SHAME	69
MICHELANGELO'S KISS	70
THE VASE OF LIFE	71
LIFE THE BELOVED	71
A SUPERSCRIPTION	72
HE AND I	73
NEWBORN DEATH	73
THE ONE HOPE	75

PART I. YOUTH AND CHANGE

INTRODUCTORY SONNET

A Sonnet is a moment's monument,—
Memorial from the Soul's eternity
To one dead deathless hour. Look that it be,
Whether for lustral rite or dire portent,
Of its own arduous fulness reverent:
Carve it in ivory or in ebony,
As Day or Night may rule; and let Time see
Its flowering crest impearled and orient.

A Sonnet is a coin: its face reveals
The soul,—its converse, to what Power 'tis due:—
Whether for tribute to the august appeals
Of Life, or dower in Love's high retinue,
It serve; or, 'mid the dark wharf's cavernous breath,
In Charon's palm it pay the toll to Death.

LOVE ENTHRONED

I marked all kindred Powers the heart finds fair:—
Truth, with awed lips; and Hope, with eyes upcast;
And Fame, whose loud wings fan the ashen Past
To signal-fires, Oblivion's flight to scare;
And Youth, with still some single golden hair
Unto his shoulder clinging, since the last
Embrace wherein two sweet arms held him fast;
And Life, still wreathing flowers for Death to wear.

Love's throne was not with these; but far above
All passionate wind of welcome and farewell
He sat in breathless bowers they dream not of;
Though Truth foreknow Love's heart, and Hope foretell,
And Fame be for Love's sake desirable,
And Youth be dear, and Life be sweet to Love.

BRIDAL BIRTH

As when desire, long darkling, dawns, and first
The mother looks upon the new-born child,
Even so my Lady stood at gaze and smiled
When her soul knew at length the Love it nursed.
Born with her life, creature of poignant thirst
And exquisite hunger, at her heart Love lay

Quickening in darkness, till a voice that day
Cried on him, and the bonds of birth were burst.

Now, shielded in his wings, our faces yearn
Together, as his fullgrown feet now range
The grove, and his warm hands our couch prepare:
Till to his song our bodiless souls in turn
Be born his children, when Death's nuptial change
Leaves us for light the halo of his hair.

REDEMPTION

O Thou who at Love's hour ecstatically
Unto my lips dost evermore present
The body and blood of Love in sacrament;
Whom I have neared and felt thy breath to be
The inmost incense of his sanctuary;
Who without speech hast owned him, and intent
Upon his will, thy life with mine hast blent,
And murmured o'er the cup, Remember me!—

0 what from thee the grace, for me the prize,
And what to Love the glory,—when the whole
Of the deep stair thou tread'st to the dim shoal
And weary water of the place of sighs,
And there dost work deliverance, as thine eyes
Draw up my prisoned spirit to thy soul!

LOVESIGHT

When do I see thee most, beloved one?
When in the light the spirits of mine eyes
Before thy face, their altar, solemnize
The worship of that Love through thee made known?
Or when in the dusk hours, (we two alone,)
Close-kissed and eloquent of still replies
Thy twilight-hidden glimmering visage lies,
And my soul only sees thy soul its own?

0 love, my love! if I no more should see
Thyself, nor on the earth the shadow of thee,
Nor image of thine eyes in any spring,—
How then should sound upon Life's darkening slope
The ground-whirl of the perished leaves of Hope,
The wind of Death's imperishable wing?

HEART'S HOPE

By what word's power, the key of paths untrod,
Shall I the difficult deeps of Love explore,
Till parted waves of Song yield up the shore
Even as that sea which Israel crossed dry-shod?
For lo! in some poor rhythmic period,
Lady, I fain would tell how evermore

Thy soul I know not from thy body, nor
Thee from myself, neither our love from God.

Yea, in God's name, and Love's, and thine, would I
Draw from one loving heart such evidence
As to all hearts all things shall signify;
Tender as dawn's first hill-fire, and intense
As instantaneous penetrating sense,
In Spring's birth-hour, of other Springs gone by.

THE KISS

What smouldering senses in death's sick delay
Or seizure of malign vicissitude
Can rob this body of honour, or denude
This soul of wedding-raiment worn to-day?
For lo! even now my lady's lips did play
With these my lips such consonant interlude
As laurelled Orpheus longed for when he wooed
The half-drawn hungering face with that last lay.

I was a child beneath her touch,—a man
When breast to breast we clung, even I and she,—
A spirit when her spirit looked through me,—
A god when all our life-breath met to fan
Our life-blood, till love's emulous ardours ran,
Fire within fire, desire in deity.

NUPTIAL SLEEP

At length their long kiss severed, with sweet smart:
And as the last slow sudden drops are shed
From sparkling eaves when all the storm has fled,
So singly flagged the pulses of each heart.
Their bosoms sundered, with the opening start
Of married flowers to either side outspread
From the knit stem; yet still their mouths, burnt red,
Fawned on each other where they lay apart.

Sleep sank them lower than the tide of dreams,
And their dreams watched them sink, and slid away.
Slowly their souls swam up again, through gleams
Of watered light and dull drowned waifs of day;
Till from some wonder of new woods and streams
He woke, and wondered more: for there she lay.

SUPREME SURRENDER

0 all the spirits of love that wander by
Along the love-sown fallowfield of sleep
My lady lies apparent; and the deep
Calls to the deep; and no man sees but I.
The bliss so long afar, at length so nigh,
Rests there attained. Methinks proud Love must weep

When Fate's control doth from his harvest reap
The sacred hour for which the years did sigh.

First touched, the hand now warm around my neck
Taught memory long to mock desire: and lo!
Across my breast the abandoned hair doth flow,
Where one shorn tress long stirred the longing ache:
And next the heart that trembled for its sake
Lies the queen-heart in sovereign overthrow.

LOVE'S LOVERS

Some ladies love the jewels in Love's zone
And gold-tipped darts he hath for painless play
In idle scornful hours he flings away;
And some that listen to his lure's soft tone
Do love to deem the silver praise their own;
Some prize his blindfold sight; and there be they
Who kissed his wings which brought him yesterday
And thank his wings to-day that he is flown.

My lady only loves the heart of Love:
Therefore Love's heart, my lady, hath for thee
His bower of unimagined flower and tree:
There kneels he now, and all-anhungered of
Thine eyes grey-lit in shadowing hair above,
Seals with thy mouth his immortality.

PASSION AND WORSHIP

One flame-winged brought a white-winged harp-player
Even where my lady and I lay all alone;
Saying: 'Behold, this minstrel is unknown;
Bid him depart, for I am minstrel here:
Only my strains are to Love's dear ones, dear.'
Then said I: 'Through thine hautboy;s rapturous tone
Unto my lady still this harp makes moan,
And still she deems the cadence deep and clear.'

Then said my,lady: 'Thou art Passion of Love,
And this Love s Worship: both he plights to me.
Thy mastering music walks the sunlit sea:
But where wan water trembles in the grove
And the wan moon is all the light thereof,
This harp still makes my name its voluntary.'

THE PORTRAIT

O Lord of all compassionate control,
0 Love! let this my lady's picture glow
Under my hand to praise her name, and show
Even of her inner self the perfect whole:
That he who seeks her beauty's furthest goal,
Beyond the light that the sweet glances throw

And refluent wave of the sweet smile, may know
The very sky and sea-line of her soul.

Lo! it is done. Above the long lithe throat
The mouth's mould testifies of voice and kiss,
The shadowed eyes remember and foresee.
Her face is made her shrine. Let all men note
That in all years (0 Love, thy gift is this!)
They that would look on her must come to me.

THE LOVE-LETTER

Warmed by her hand and shadowed by her hair
As close she leaned and poured her heart through thee,
Whereof the articulate throbs accompany
The smooth black stream that makes thy whiteness fair,—
Sweet fluttering sheet, even of her breath aware,—
Oh let thy silent song disclose to me
That soul wherewith her lips and eyes agree
Like married music in Love's answering air.

Fain had I watched her when, at some fond thought,
Her bosom to the writing closelier press'd,
And her breast's secrets peered into her breast;
When, through eyes raised an instant, her soul sought
My soul, and from the sudden confluence caught
The words that made her love the loveliest.

THE LOVERS' WALK

Sweet twining hedgeflowers wind-stirred in no wise
On this June day; and hand that clings in hand:—
Still glades; and meeting faces scarcely fann'd:—
An osier-odoured stream that draws the skies
Deep to its heart; and mirrored eyes in eyes:—
Fresh hourly wonder o'er the Summer land
Of light and cloud; and two souls softly spann'd
With one o'erarching heaven of smiles and sighs:—

Even such their path, whose bodies lean unto
Each other's visible sweetness amorously,—
Whose passionate hearts lean by Love's high decree
Together on his heart for ever true,
As the cloud-foaming firmamental blue
Rests on the blue line of a foamless sea.

ANTIPHONY

'I love you, sweet: how can you ever learn
How much I love you?' 'You I love even so,
And so I learn it.' 'Sweet, you cannot know
How fair you are.' 'If fair enough to earn
Your love, so much is all my love's concern.'
'My love grows hourly, sweet.' ' Mine too doth grow,

Yet love seemed full so many hours ago!'
Thus lovers speak, till kisses claim their turn.

Ah! happy they to whom such words as these
In youth have served for speech the whole day long,
Hour after hour, remote from the world's throng,
Work, contest, fame, all life's confederate pleas,—
What while Love breathed in sighs and silences
Through two blent souls one rapturous undersong.

YOUTH'S SPRING-TRIBUTE

On this sweet bank your head thrice sweet and dear
I lay, and spread your hair on either side,
And see the newborn wood flowers bashful-eyed
Look through the golden tresses here and there.
On these debateable borders of the year
Spring's foot half falters; scarce she yet may know
The leafless blackthorn-blossom from the snow;
And through her bowers the wind's way still is clear.

But April's sun strikes down the glades to-day;
So shut your eyes upturned, and feel my kiss
Creep, as the Spring now thrills through every spray,
Up your warm throat to your warm lips: for this
Is even the hour of Love's sworn suitservice,
With whom cold hearts are counted castaway.

THE BIRTH-BOND

Havw you not noted, in some family
Where two were born of a first marriage-bed,
How still they own their gracious bond, though fed
And nursed on the forgotten breast and knee?—
How to their father's children they shall be
In act and thought of one goodwill; but each
Shall for the other have, in silence speech,
And in a word complete community?

Even so, when first I saw you, seemed it, love,
That among souls allied to mine was yet
One nearer kindred than life hinted of.
0 born with me somewhere that men forget,
And though in years of sight and sound unmet,
Known for my soul's birth-partner well enough!

A DAY OF LOVE

Those envied places which do know her well,
And are so scornful of this lonely place,
Even now for once are emptied of her grace:
Nowhere but here she is: and while Love's spell
From his predominant presence doth compel
All alien hours, an outworn populace,

The hours of Love fill full the echoing space
With sweet confederate music favourable.

Now many memories make solicitous
The delicate love-lines of her mouth, till, lit
With quivering fire, the words take wing from it;
As here between our kisses we sit thus
Speaking of things remembered, and so sit
Speechless while things forgotten call to us.

BEAUTY'S PAGEANT

What dawn-pulse at the heart of heaven, or last
Incarnate flower of culminating day,—
What marshalled marvels on the skirts of May,
Or song full-quired, sweet June's encomiast;
What glory of change by nature's hand amass'd
Can vie with all those moods of varying grace
Which o'er one loveliest woman's form and face
Within this hour, within this room, have pass'd?

Love's very vesture and elect disguise
Was each fine movement,—wonder new-begot
Of lily or swan or swan-stemmed galiot;
Joy to his sight who now the sadlier sighs,
Parted again; and sorrow yet for eyes
Unborn that read these words and saw her not.

GENIUS IN BEAUTY

Beauty like hers is genius. Not the call
Of Homer's or of Dante's heart sublime,—
Not Michael's hand furrowing the zones of time,—
Is more with compassed mysteries musical;
Nay, not in Spring's or Summer's sweet footfall
More gathered gifts exuberant Life bequeathes
Than doth this sovereign face, whose love-spell breathes
Even from its shadowed contour on the wall.

As many men are poets in their youth,
But for one sweet-strung soul the wires prolong
Even through all change the indomitable song;
So in likewise the envenomed years, whose tooth
Rends shallower grace with ruin void of ruth,
Upon this beauty's power shall wreak no wrong.

SILENT NOON

Your hands lie open in the long fresh grass,—
The finger-points look through the rosy blooms:
Your eyes smile peace. The pasture gleams and glooms
'Neath billowing skies that scatter and amass.
All round our nest, far as the eye can pass,
Are golden kingcup-fields with silver edge

Where the cow-parsley skirts the hawthorn-hedge.
'Tis visible silence, still as the hour-glass.

Deep in the sun-searched growths the dragon-fly
Hangs like a blue thread loosened from the sky:
So this wing'd hour is dropt to us from above.
Oh! clasp we to our hearts, for deathless dower,
This close-companioned inarticulate hour
When twofold silence was the song of love.

GRACIOUS MOONLIGHT

Even as the moon grows queenlier in mid-space
When the sky darkens, and her cloud-rapt car
Thrills with intenser radiance from afar,—
So lambent, lady, beams thy sovereign grace
When the drear soul desires thee. Of that face
What shall be said,—which, like a governing star,
Gathers and garners from all things that are
Their silent penetrative loveliness?

O'er water-daisies and wild waifs of Spring,
There where the iris rears its gold-crowned sheaf
With flowering rush and sceptred arrow-leaf,
So have I marked Queen Dian, in bright ring
Of cloud above and wave below, take wing
And chase night's gloom, as thou the spirit's grief.

LOVE-SWEETNESS

Sweet dimness of her loosened hair's downfall
About thy face; her sweet hands round thy head
In gracious fostering union garlanded,
Her tremulous smiles, her glances' sweet recall
Of love; her murmuring sighs memorial;
Her mouth's culled sweetness by thy kisses shed
On cheeks and neck and eyelids, and so led
Back to her mouth which answers there for all:—

What sweeter than these things, except the thing
In lacking which all these would lose their sweet:—
The confident heart's still fervour: the swift beat
And soft subsidence of the spirit's wing,
Then when it feels, in cloud—girt wayfaring,
The breath of kindred plumes against its feet?

HEART'S HAVEN

Sometimes she is a child within mine arms,
Cowering beneath dark wings that love must chase,—
With still tears showering and averted face,
Inexplicably filled with faint alarms:
And oft from mine own spirit's hurtling harms
I crave the refuge of her deep embrace,—

Against all ills the fortified strong place
And sweet reserve of sovereign counter-charms.

And Love, our light at night and shade at noon,
Lulls us to rest with songs, and turns away
All shafts of shelterless tumultuous day.
Like the moon's growth, his face gleams through his tune;
And as soft waters warble to the moon,
Our answering spirits chime one roundelay.

LOVE'S BAUBLES

I stood where Love in brimming armfuls bore
Slight wanton flowers and foolish toys of fruit:
And round him ladies thronged in warm pursuit,
Fingered and lipped and proffered the strange store:
And from one hand the petal and the core
Savoured of sleep; and cluster and curled shoot
Seemed from another hand like shame's salute,—
Gifts that I felt my cheek was blushing for.

At last Love bade my Lady give the same:
And as I looked, the dew was light thereon;
And as I took them, at her touch they shone
With inmost heaven-hue of the heart of flame.
And then Love said: 'Lo! when the hand is hers,
Follies of love are love's true ministers.'

PRIDE OF YOUTH

Even as a child, of sorrow that we give
The dead, but little in his heart can find,
Since without need of thought to his clear mind
Their turn it is to die and his to live:
Even so the winged New Love smiles to receive
Along his eddying plumes the auroral wind,
Nor, forward glorying, casts one look behind
Where night-rack shrouds the Old Love fugitive.

There is a change in every hour's recall,
And the last cowslip in the fields we see
On the same day with the first corn-poppy.
Alas for hourly change! Alas for all
The loves that from his hand proud Youth lets fall,
Even as the beads of a told rosary!

WINGED HOURS

Each hour until we meet is as a bird
That wings from far his gradual way along
The rustling covert of my soul,—his song
Still loudlier trilled through leaves more deeply stirr'd:
But at the hour of meeting, a clear word
Is every note he sings, in Love's own tongue;

Yet, Love, thou know'st the sweet strain wrong,
Through our contending kisses oft unheard.

What of that hour at last, when for her sake
No wing may fly to me nor song may flow;
When, wandering round my life unleaved, I
The bloodied feathers scattered in the brake,
And think how she, far from me, with like eyes
Sees through the untuneful bough the wingless skies?

MID – RAPTURE

Thou lovely and beloved, thou my love;
Whose kiss seems still the first; whose summoning eyes,
Even now, as for our love-world's new sunrise,
Shed very dawn; whose voice, attuned above
All modulation of the deep-bowered dove,
Is like a hand laid softly on the soul;
Whose hand is like a sweet voice to control
Those worn tired brows it hath the keeping of:—

What word can answer to thy word,—what gaze
To thine, which now absorbs within its sphere
My worshipping face, till I am mirrored there
Light-circled in a heaven of deep-drawn rays?
What clasp, what kiss mine inmost heart can prove,
0 lovely and beloved, 0 my love?

HEART'S COMPASS

Sometimes thou seem'st not as thyself alone,
But as the meaning of all things that are;
A breathless wonder, shadowing forth afar
Some heavenly solstice hushed and halcyon;
Whose unstirred lips are music's visible tone;
Whose eyes the sun-gate of the soul unbar,
Being of its furthest fires oracular;—
The evident heart of all life sown and mown.

Even such Love is; and is not thy name Love?
Yea, by thy hand the Love-god rends apart
All gathering clouds of Night's ambiguous art;
Flings them far down, and sets thine eyes above;
And simply, as some gage of flower or glove,
Stakes with a smile the world against thy heart.

SOUL-LIGHT

What other woman could be loved like you,
Or how of you should love possess his fill?
After the fulness of all rapture, still,—
As at the end of some deep avenue
A tender glamour of day,—there comes to view
Far in your eyes a yet more hungering thrill,—

Such fire as Love's soul-winnowing hands distil
Even from his inmost arc of light and dew.

And as the traveller triumphs with the sun,
Glorying in heat's mid-height, yet startide brings
Wonder new-born, and still fresh transport springs
From limpid lambent hours of day begun;—
Even so, through eyes and voice, your soul doth move
My soul with changeful light of infinite love.

THE MOONSTAR

Lady, I thank thee for thy loveliness,
Because my lady is more lovely still.
Glorying I gaze, and yield with glad goodwill
To thee thy tribute; by whose sweet-spun dress
Of delicate life Love labours to assess
My Lady's absolute queendom; saying, 'Lo!
How high this beauty is, which yet doth show
But as that beauty's sovereign votaress.'

Lady, I saw thee with her, side by side;
And as, when night's fair fires their queen surround,
An emulous star too near the moon will ride,—
Even so thy rays within her luminous bound
Were traced no more; and by the light so drown'd,
Lady, not thou but she was glorified.

LAST FIRE

Love, through your spirit and mine what summer eve
Now glows with glory of all things possess'd,
Since this day's sun of rapture filled the west
And the light sweetened as the fire took leave?
Awhile now softlier let your bosom heave,
As in Love's harbour, even that loving breast,
All care takes refuge while we sink to rest,
And mutual dreams the bygone bliss retrieve.

Many the days that Winter keeps in store,
Sunless throughout, or whose brief sun-glimpses
Scarce shed the heaped snow through the naked trees.
This day at least was Summer's paramour,
Sun-coloured to the imperishable core
With sweet well-being of love and full heart's ease.

HER GIFTS

High grace, the dower of queens; and therewithal
Some wood-born wonder's sweet simplicity;
A glance like water brimming with the sky
Or hyacinth-light where forest-shadows fall;
Such thrilling pallor of cheek as doth enthral
The heart; a mouth whose passionate forms imply

All music and all silence held thereby;
Deep golden locks, her sovereign coronal;
A round reared neck, meet column of Love's shrine
To cling to when the heart takes sanctuary;
Hands which for ever at Love's bidding be,
And soft-stirred feet still answering to his sign:—
These are her gifts, as tongue may tell them o'er.
Breathe low her name, my soul; for that means more.

EQUAL TROTH

Not by one measure mayst thou mete our love;
For how should I be loved as I love thee?—
I, graceless, joyless, lacking absolutely
 All gifts that with thy queenship best behove;—
Thou, throned in every heart's elect alcove,
And crowned with garlands culled from every tree,
Which for no head but thine, by Love's decree,
All beauties and all mysteries interwove.

But here thine eyes and lips yield soft rebuke:—
'Then only,' (say'st thou), 'could I love thee less,
When thou couldst doubt my love's equality.'
Peace, sweet! If not to sum but worth we look,
Thy heart's transcendence, not my heart's excess,
Then more a thousandfold thou lov'st than I.

VENUS VICTRIX

Could Juno's self more sovereign presence wear
Than thou, 'mid other ladies throned in grace?—
Or Pallas, when thou bend'st with soul-stilled face
O'er poet's page gold-shadowed in thy hair?
Dost thou than Venus seem less heavenly fair
When o'er the sea of love's tumultuous trance
Hovers thy smile, and mingles with thy glance
That sweet voice like the last wave murmuring there?

Before such triune loveliness divine
Awestruck I ask, which goddess here most claims
The prize that, howsoe'er adjudged, is thine?
Then Love breathes low the sweetest of thy names;
And Venus Victrix to my heart doth bring
Herself, the Helen of her guerdoning.

THE DARK GLASS

Not I myself know all my love for thee:
How should I reach so far, who cannot weigh
To-morrow's dower by gage of yesterday?
Shall birth and death, and all dark names that be
As doors and windows bared to some loud sea,
Lash deaf mine ears and blind my face with spray;

And shall my sense pierce love,—the last relay
And ultimate outpost of eternity?

Lo! what am I to Love, the lord of all?
One murmuring shell he gathers from the sand,—
One little heart-flame sheltered in his hand.
Yet through thine eyes he grants me clearest call
And veriest touch of powers primordial
That any hour-girt life may understand.

THE LAMP'S SHRINE

Sometimes I fain would find in thee some fault,
That I might love thee still in spite of it:
Yet how should our Lord Love curtail one whit
Thy perfect praise whom most he would exalt?
Alas! he can but make my heart's low vault
Even in men's sight unworthier, being lit
By thee, who thereby show'st more exquisite
Like fiery chrysoprase in deep basalt.

Yet will I nowise shrink; but at Love's shrine
Myself within the beams his brow doth dart
Will set the flashing jewel of thy heart
In that dull chamber where it deigns to shine:
For lo! in honour of thine excellencies
My heart takes pride to show how poor it is.

LIFE – IN – LOVE

Not in thy body is thy life at all
But in this lady's lips and hands and eyes;
Through these she yields the life that vivifies
What else were sorrow's servant and death's thrall.
Look on thyself without her, and recall
The waste remembrance and forlorn surmise
That lived but in a dead-drawn breath of sighs
O'er vanished hours and hours eventual.

Even so much life hath the poor tress of hair
Which, stored apart, is all love hath to show
For heart-beats and for fire-heats long ago;
Even so much life endures unknown, even where,
'Mid change the changeless night environeth,
Lies all that golden hair undimmed in death.

THE LOVE – MOON

'When that dead face, bowered in the furthest years,
Which once was all the life years held for thee,
Can now scarce bide the tides of memory
Cast on thy soul a little spray of tears,—
How canst thou gaze into these eyes of hers
Whom now thy heart delights in, and not see

Within each orb Love's philtred euphrasy
Make them of buried troth remembrancers?'

'Nay, pitiful Love, nay, loving Pity! Well
Thou knowest that in these twain I have confess'd
Two very voices of thy summoning bell.
Nay, Master, shall not Death make manifest
In these the culminant changes which approve
The love-moon that must light my soul to Love?'

THE MORROW'S MESSAGE

'Thou Ghost,' I said, 'and is thy name To-day?—
Yesterday's son, with such an abject brow!—
And can To-morrow be more pale than thou?'
While yet I spoke, the silence answered: 'Yea,
Henceforth our issue is all grieved and grey,
And each beforehand makes such poor avow
As of old leaves beneath the budding bough
Or night-drift that the sundawn shreds away.'

Then cried I: 'Mother of many malisons,
0 Earth, receive me to thy dusty bed!'
But therewithal the tremulous silence said:
'Lo! Love yet bids thy lady greet thee once:—
Yea, twice, – whereby thy life is still the sun's;
And thrice, — whereby the shadow of death is dead.'

SLEEPLESS DREAMS

Girt in dark growths, yet glimmering with one star,
0 night desirous as the nights of youth!
Why should my heart within thy spell, forsooth,
Now beat, as the bride's finger-pulses are
Quickened within the girdling golden bar?
What wings are these that fan my pillow smooth?
And why does Sleep, waved back by Joy and Ruth,
Tread softly round and gaze at me from far?

Nay, night deep-leaved! And would Love feign in thee
Some shadowy palpitating grove that bears
Rest for man's eyes and music for his ears?
0 lonely night! art thou not known to me,
A thicket hung with masks of mockery
And watered with the wasteful warmth of tears?

SEVERED SELVES

Two separate divided silences,
Which, brought together, would find loving voice;
Two glances which together would rejoice
In love, now lost like stars beyond dark trees;
Two hands apart whose touch alone gives ease;
Two bosoms which, heart-shrined with mutual flame,

Would, meeting in one clasp, be made the same;
Two souls, the shores wave-mocked of sundering seas:—

Such are we now. Ah! may our hope forecast
Indeed one hour again, when on this stream
Of darkened love once more the light shall gleam?
An hour how slow to come, how quickly past,
Which blooms and fades, and only leaves at last,
Faint as shed flowers, the attenuated dream.

THROUGH DEATH TO LOVE

Like labour-laden moonclouds faint to flee
From winds that sweep the winter-bitten wold,—
Like multiform circumfluence manifold
Of night's flood-tide,—like terrors that agree
Of hoarse-tongued fire and inarticulate sea,—
Even such, within some glass dimmed by our breath,
Our hearts discern wild images of Death,
Shadows and shoals that edge eternity.

Howbeit athwart Death's imminent shade doth soar
One Power, than flow of stream or flight of dove
Sweeter to glide around, to brood above.
Tell me, my heart;—what angel-greeted door
Or threshold of wing-winnowed threshing-floor
Hath guest fire-fledged as thine, whose lord is Love?

HOPE OVERTAKEN

I deemed thy garments, O my Hope, were grey,
So far I viewed thee. Now the space between
Is passed at length; and garmented in green
Even as in days of yore thou stand'st to-day.
Ah God! and but for lingering dull dismay,
On all that road our footsteps erst had been
Even thus commingled, and our shadows seen
Blent on the hedgerows and the water-way.

O Hope of mine whose eyes are living love,
No eyes but hers,—O Love and Hope the same!—
Lean close to me, for now the sinking sun
That warmed our feet scarce gilds our hair above.
O hers thy voice and very hers thy name!
Alas, cling round me, for the day is done!

LOVE AND HOPE

Bless love and hope. Full many a withered year
Whirled past us, eddying to its chill doomsday;
And clasped together where the blown leaves lay,
We long have knelt and wept full many a tear.
Yet lo! one hour at last, the Spring's compeer,
Flutes softly to us from some green byeway:

Those years, those tears are dead, but only they:—
Bless love and hope, true soul; for we are here.

Cling heart to heart; nor of this hour demand
Whether in very truth, when we are dead,
Our hearts shall wake to know Love's golden head
Sole sunshine of the imperishable land;
Or but discern, through night's unfeatured scope,
Scorn-fired at length the illusive eyes of Hope.

CLOUD AND WIND

Love, should I fear death most for you or me?
Yet if you die, can I not follow you,
Forcing the straits of change? Alas! but who
Shall wrest a bond from night's inveteracy,
Ere yet my hazardous soul put forth, to be
Her warrant against all her haste might rue?—
Ah! in your eyes so reached what dumb adieu,
What unsunned gyres of waste eternity?

And if I die the first, shall death be then
A lampless watchtower whence I see you weep?—
Or (woe is me!) a bed wherein my sleep
Ne'er notes (as death s dear cup at last you drain),
The hour when you too learn that all is vain
And that Hope sows what Love shall never reap?

SECRET PARTING

Because our talk was of the cloud-control
And moon-track of the journeying face of Fate,
Her tremulous kisses faltered at love's gate
And her eyes dreamed against a distant goal:
But soon, remembering her how brief the whole
Of joy, which its own hours annihilate,
Her set gaze gathered, thirstier than of late,
And as she kissed, her mouth became her soul.

Thence in what ways we wandered, and how strove
To build with fire-tried vows the piteous home
Which memory haunts and whither sleep may roam,—
They only know for whom the roof of Love
Is the still-seated secret of the grove,
Nor spire may rise nor bell be heard therefrom.

PARTED LOVE

What shall be said of this embattled day
And armed occupation of this night
By all thy foes beleaguered,—now when sight
Nor sound denotes the loved one far away?
Of these thy vanquished hours what shalt thou say,—
As every sense to which she dealt delight

Now labours lonely o'er the stark noon-height
To reach the sunset's desolate disarray?

Stand still, fond fettered wretch! while Memory's art
Parades the Past before thy face, and lures
Thy spirit to her passionate portraitures:
Till the tempestuous tide-gates flung apart
Flood with wild will the hollows of thy heart,
And thy heart rends thee, and thy body endures.

BROKEN MUSIC

The mother will not turn, who thinks she hears
Her nursling's speech first grow articulate;
But breathless with averted eyes elate
She sits, with open lips and open ears,
That it may call her twice. 'Mid doubts and fears
Thus oft my soul has hearkened; till the song,
A central moan for days, at length found tongue,
And the sweet music welled and the sweet tears.

But now, whatever while the soul is fain
To list that wonted murmur, as it were
The speech-bound sea-shell's low importunate strain,—
No breath of song, thy voice alone is there,
O bitterly beloved! and all her gain
Is but the pang of unpermitted prayer.

DEATH-IN-LOVE

There came an image in Life's retinue
That had Love's wings and bore his gonfalon:
Fair was the web, and nobly wrought thereon,
0 soul-sequestered face, thy form and hue!
Bewildering sounds, such as Spring wakens to,
Shook in its folds; and through my heart its power
Sped trackless as the immemorial hour
When birth's dark portal groaned and all was new.

But a veiled woman followed, and she caught
The banner round its staff, to furl and cling,—
Then plucked a feather from the bearer's wing,
And held it to his lips that stirred it not,
And said to me, 'Behold, there is no breath:
I and this Love are one, and I am Death.'

WILLOWWOOD

I

I sat with Love upon a woodside well,
Leaning across the water, I and he;
Nor ever did he speak nor looked at me,
But touched his lute wherein was audible
The certain secret thing he had to tell:

Only our mirrored eyes met silently
In the low wave; and that sound came to be
The passionate voice I knew; and my tears fell.

And at their fall, his eyes beneath grew hers;
And with his foot and with his wing-feathers
He swept the spring that watered my heart's drouth.
Then the dark ripples spread to waving hair,
And as I stooped, her own lips rising there
Bubbled with brimming kisses at my mouth.

II

And now Love sang: but his was such a song,
So meshed with half-remembrance hard to free,
As souls disused in death's sterility
May sing when the new birthday tarries long.
And I was made aware of a dumb throng
That stood aloof, one form by every tree,
All mournful forms, for each was I or she,
The shades of those our days that had no tongue.

They looked on us, and knew us and were known;
While fast together, alive from the abyss,
Clung the soul-wrung implacable close kiss;
And pity of self through all made broken moan
Which said, 'For once, for once, for once alone!'
And still Love sang, and what he sang was this:—

III

'O ye, all ye that walk in Willow-wood,
That walk with hollow faces burning white;
What fathom-depth of soul-struck widowhood,
What long, what longer hours, one lifelong night,
Ere ye again, who so in vain have wooed
Your last hope lost, who so in vain invite
Your lips to that their unforgotten food,
Ere ye, ere ye again shall see the light!

Alas! the bitter banks in Willowwood,
With tear-spurge wan, with blood-wort burning red:
Alas! if ever such a pillow could
Steep deep the soul in sleep till she were dead,—
Better all life forget her than this thing,
That Willowwood should hold her wandering!'

IV

So sang he: and as meeting rose and rose
Together cling through the wind's wellaway
Nor change at once, yet near the end of day
The leaves drop loosened where the heart-stain glows,—
So when the song died did the kiss unclose;
And her face fell back drowned, and was as grey
As its grey eyes; and if it ever may
Meet mine again I know not if Love knows.

Only I know that I leaned low and drank
A long draught from the water where she sank,

Her breath and all her tears and all her soul:
And as I leaned, I know I felt Love's face
Pressed on my neck with moan of pity and grace,
Till both our heads were in his aureole.

WITHOUT HER

What of her glass without her? The blank grey
There where the pool is blind of the moon's face.
Her dress without her? The tossed empty space
Of cloud-rack whence the moon has passed away.
Her paths without her? Day's appointed sway
Usurped by desolate night. Her pillowed place
Without her? Tears, ah me! for love's good grace,
And cold forgetfulness of night or day.

What of the heart without her? Nay, poor heart,
Of thee what word remains ere speech be still?
A wayfarer by barren ways and chill,
Steep ways and weary, without her thou art,
Where the long cloud, the long wood's counterpart,
Sheds doubled darkness up the labouring hill.

LOVE'S FATALITY

Sweet Love,— but oh! most dread Desire of Love
Life-thwarted. Linked in gyves I saw them stand,
Love shackled with Vain-longing, hand to hand:
And one was eyed as the blue vault above:
But hope tempestuous like a fire-cloud hove
I' the other s gaze, even as in his whose wand
Vainly all night with spell-wrought power has spann'd
The unyielding caves of some deep treasure-trove.

Also his lips, two writhen flakes of flame,
Made moan: 'Alas 0 Love, thus leashed with me!
Wing-footed thou, wing-shouldered, once born free:
And I, thy cowering self, in chains grown tame,
Bound to thy body and soul, named with thy name,
Life's iron heart, even Love's Fatality.'

STILLBORN LOVE

The hour which might have been yet might not be,
Which man's and woman's heart conceived and bore
Yet whereof life was barren,—on what shore
Bides it the breaking of Time's weary sea?
Bondchild of all consummate joys set free,
It somewhere sighs and serves, and mute before

The house of Love, hears through the echoing door
His hours elect in choral consonancy.

But lo! what wedded souls now hand in hand
Together tread at last the immortal strand
With eyes where burning memory lights love home?
Lo! how the little outcast hour has turned
And leaped to them and in their faces yearned: —
'I am your child: 0 parents, ye have come!'

TRUE WOMAN

I. HERSELF

To be a sweetness more desired than Spring;
A bodily beauty more acceptable
Than the wild rose-tree's arch that crowns the fell;
To be an essence more environing
Than wine's drained juice; a music ravishing
More than the passionate pulse of Philomel; –
To be all this 'neath one soft bosom's swell
That is the flower of life:—how strange a thing!

How strange a thing to be what Man can know
But as a sacred secret! Heaven's own screen
Hides her soul's purest depth and loveliest glow;
Closely withheld, as all things most unseen,—
The wave-bowered pearl, the heart-shaped seal of green
That flecks the snowdrop underneath the snow.

II. HER LOVE

She loves him; for her infinite soul is Love,
And he her lodestar. Passion in her is
A glass facing his fire, where the bright bliss
Is mirrored, and the heat returned. Yet move
That glass, a stranger's amorous flame to prove,
And it shall turn, by instant contraries,
Ice to the moon; while her pure fire to his
For whom it burns, clings close i' the heart's alcove.

Lo! they are one. With wifely breast to breast
And circling arms, she welcomes all command
Of love,—her soul to answering ardours fann'd:
Yet as morn springs or twilight sinks to rest,
Ah! who shall say she deems not loveliest
The hour of sisterly sweet hand-in-hand?

III. HER HEAVEN

If to grow old in Heaven is to grow young,
(As the Seer saw and said,) then blest were he
With youth forevermore, whose heaven should be
True Woman, she whom these weak notes have sung.
Here and hereafter,—choir-strains of her tongue,—
Sky-spaces of her eyes,—sweet signs that flee
About her soul's immediate sanctuary,—
Were Paradise all uttermost worlds among.

The sunrise blooms and withers on the hill
Like any hillflower; and the noblest troth
Dies here to dust. Yet shall Heaven's promise clothe

Even yet those lovers who have cherished still
This test for love:—in every kiss sealed fast
To feel the first kiss and forebode the last.

LOVE'S LAST GIFT

Love to his singer held a glistening leaf,
And said: 'The rose-tree and the apple-tree
Have fruits to vaunt or flowers to lure the bee;
And golden shafts are in the feathered sheaf
Of the great harvest-marshal, the year's chief,
Victorious Summer; aye, and 'neath warm sea
Strange secret grasses lurk inviolably
Between the filtering channels of sunk reef.

All are my blooms; and all sweet blooms of love
To thee I gave while Spring and Summer sang;
But Autumn stops to listen, with some pang
From those worse things the wind is moaning of.
Only this laurel dreads no winter days:
Take my last gift; thy heart hath sung my praise.'

PART II. CHANGE AND FATE

TRANSFIGURED LIFE

As growth of form or momentary glance
In a child's features will recall to mind
The father's with the mother's face combin'd,—
Sweet interchange that memories still enhance:
And yet, as childhood's years and youth's advance,
The gradual mouldings leave one stamp behind,
Till in the blended likeness now we find
A separate man's or woman's countenance:—

So in the Song, the singer's Joy and Pain,
Its very parents, evermore expand
To bid the passion's fullgrown birth remain,
By Art's transfiguring essence subtly spann'd;
And from that song-cloud shaped as a man's hand
There comes the sound as of abundant rain.

THE SONG-THROE

By thine own tears thy song must tears beget,
O Singer! Magic mirror thou hast none
Except thy manifest heart; and save thine own
Anguish or ardour, else no amulet.
Cisterned in Pride, verse is the feathery jet
Of soulless air-flung fountains; nay, more dry
Than the Dead Sea for throats that thirst and sigh,
That song o'er which no singer's lids grew wet.

The Song-god—He the Sun-god—is no slave
Of thine: thy Hunter he, who for thy soul
Fledges his shaft: to no august control
Of thy skilled hand his quivered store he gave:
But if thy lips' loud cry leap to his smart,
The inspir'd recoil shall pierce thy brother's heart.

THE SOUL'S SPHERE

Come prisoned moon in steep cloud-fastnesses,—
Throned queen and thralled; some dying sun whose pyre
Blazed with momentous memorable fire;—
Who hath not yearned and fed his heart with these?
Who, sleepless, hath not anguished to appease
Tragical shadow's realm of sound and sight

Conjectured in the lamentable night?...
Lo! the soul's sphere of infinite images!

What sense shall count them? Whether it forecast
The rose-winged hours that flutter in the van
Of Love's unquestioning unreveale'd span,—
Visions of golden futures: or that last
Wild pageant of the accumulated past
That clangs and flashes for a drowning man.

INCLUSIVENESS

The changing guests, each in a different mood,
Sit at the roadside table and arise:
And every life among them in likewise
Is a soul's board set daily with new food.
What man has bent o'er his son's sleep, to brood
How that face shall watch his when cold it lies?—
Or thought, as his own mother kissed his eyes,
Of what her kiss was when his father wooed?

May not this ancient room thou sit'st in dwell
In separate living souls for joy or pain?
Nay, all its corners may be painted plain
Where Heaven shows pictures of some life spent well;
And may be stamped, a memory all in vain,
Upon the sight of lidless eyes in Hell.

ARDOUR AND MEMORY

The cuckoo-throb, the heartbeat of the Spring;
The rosebud's blush that leaves it as it grows
Into the full-eyed fair unblushing rose;
The summer clouds that visit every wing
With fires of sunrise and of sunsetting;
The furtive flickering streams to light re-born
'Mid airs new-fledged and valorous lusts of morn,
While all the daughters of the daybreak sing:—

These ardour loves, and memory: and when flown
All joys, and through dark forest-boughs in flight
The wind swoops onward brandishing the light,
Even yet the rose-tree's verdure left alone
Will flush all ruddy though the rose be gone;
With ditties and with dirges infinite.

KNOWN IN VAIN

As two whose love, first foolish, widening scope,
Knows suddenly, with music high and soft,
The Holy of holies; who because they scoff'd
Are now amazed with shame, nor dare to cope
With the whole truth aloud, lest heaven should ope;
Yet, at their meetings, laugh not as they

In speech; nor speak, at length; but sitting oft
Together, within hopeless sight of hope
For hours are silent:—So it happeneth
When Work and Will awake too late, to gaze
After their life sailed by, and hold their breath.
Ah! who shall dare to search through what sad maze
Thenceforth their incommunicable ways
Follow the desultory feet of Death?

HEART OF THE NIGHT

From child to youth; from youth to arduous man;
From lethargy to fever of the heart;
From faithful life to dream-dowered days apart;
From trust to doubt; from doubt to brink of ban;—
Thus much of change in one swift cycle ran
Till now. Alas, the soul!—how soon must she
Accept her primal immortality,—
The flesh resume its dust whence it began?

0 Lord of work and peace! 0 Lord of life!
0 Lord, the awful Lord of will! though late,
Even yet renew this soul with duteous breath:
That when the peace is garnered in from strife,
The work retrieved, the will regenerate,
This soul may see thy face, 0 Lord of death!

THE LANDMARK

Was *that* the landmark? What,—the foolish well
Whose wave, low down, I did not stoop to drink,
But sat and flung the pebbles from its brink
In sport to send its imaged skies pell-mell,
(And mine own image, had I noted well!)
Was that my point of turning?—I had thought
The stations of my course should rise unsought,
As altar-stone or ensigned citadel.

But lo! the path is missed, I must go back,
And thirst to drink when next I reach the spring
Which once I stained, which since may have grown black.
Yet though no light be left nor bird now sing
As here I turn, I'll thank God, hastening,
That the same goal is still on the same track.

A DARK DAY

The gloom that breathes upon me with these airs
Is like the drops which strike the traveller's brow
Who knows not, darkling, if they bring him now
Fresh storm, or be old rain the covert bears.
Ah! bodes this hour some harvest of new tares,
Or hath but memory of the day whose plough

Sowed hunger once,— the night at length when thou,
0 prayer found vain, didst fall from out my prayers?

How prickly were the growths which yet how smooth,
Along the hedgerows of this journey shed,
Lie by Time's grace till night and sleep may soothe!
Even as the thistledown from pathsides dead
Gleaned by a girl in autumns of her youth,
Which one new year makes soft her marriage-bed.

AUTUMN IDLENESS

This sunlight shames November where he grieves
In dead red leaves, and will not let him shun
The day, though bough with bough be over-run.
But with a blessing every glade receives
High salutation; while from hillock-eaves
The deer gaze calling, dappled white and dun,
As if, being foresters of old, the sun
Had marked them with the shade of forest-leaves.

Here dawn to-day unveiled her magic glass;
Here noon now gives the thirst and takes the dew;
Till eve bring rest when other good things pass.
And here the lost hours the lost hours renew
While I still lead my shadow o'er the grass,
Nor know, for longing, that which I should do.

THE HILL SUMMIT

This feast-day of the sun, his altar there
In the broad west has blazed for vesper-song;
And I have loitered in the vale too long
And gaze now a belated worshipper.
Yet may I not forget that I was 'ware,
So journeying, of his face at intervals
Transfigured where the fringed horizon falls,—
A fiery bush with coruscating hair.

And now that I have climbed and won this height,
I must tread downward through the sloping shade
And travel the bewildered tracks till night.
Yet for this hour I still may here be stayed
And see the gold air and the silver fade
And the last bird fly into the last light.

THE CHOICE

I

Eat thou and drink; to-morrow thou shalt die.
Surely the earth, that s wise being very old,
Needs not our help. Then loose me, love, and hold
Thy sultry hair up from my face that I
May pour for thee this yellow wine, brim-high,

Till round the glass thy fingers glow like gold.
We'll drown all hours: thy song, while hours toil'd,
Shall leap, as fountains veil the changing sky.

Now kiss, and think that there are really those,
My own high-bosomed beauty, who increase
Vain gold, vain lore, and yet might choose our way
Through many days they toil; then comes a day
They die not,—never having lived,—but cease;
And round their narrow lips the mould falls close.

II

Watch thou and fear; to-morrow thou shalt die.
Or art thou sure thou shalt have time for death?
Is not the day which God's word promiseth
To come man knows not when? In yonder sky,
Now while we speak, the sun speeds forth: can I
Or thou assure him of his goal? God's breath
Even at the moment haply quickeneth
The air to a flame; till spirits, always nigh
Though screened and hid, shall walk the daylight here.

And dost thou prate of all that man shall do?
Canst thou, who hast but plagues, presume to be
Glad in his gladness that comes after thee?
Will *his* strength slay *thy* worm in Hell? Go to:
Cover thy countenance, and watch, and fear. Think thou and act;
to-morrow thou shalt die.
Outstretched in the sun's warmth upon the shore,
Thou say'st: 'Man's measured path is all gone o'er:
Up all his years, steeply, with strain and sigh,
Man clomb until he touched the truth; and I,

Even I, am he whom it was destined for.'
How should this be? Art thou then so much more
Than they who sowed, that thou shouldst reap thereby?

Nay, come up hither. From this wave-washed mound
Unto the furthest flood-brim look with me;
Then reach on with thy thought till it be drown'd.
Miles and miles distant though the grey line be,
And though thy soul sail leagues and leagues beyond,—
Still, leagues beyond those leagues there is more sea.

OLD AND NEW ART

I. ST. LUKE THE PAINTER

Give honour unto Luke Evangelist;
For he it was (the aged legends say)
Who first taught Art to fold her hands and pray.
Scarcely at once she dared to rend the mist
Of devious symbols: but soon having wist
How sky-breadth and field-silence and this day
Are symbols also in some deeper way,
She looked through these to God and was God's priest.

And if, past noon, her toil began to irk,
And she sought talismans, and turned in vain
To soulless self-reflections of man's skill,
Yet now, in this the twilight, she might still

Kneel in the latter grass to pray again,
Ere the night cometh and she may not work.

II. NOT AS THESE

'I am not as these are,' the poet saith
In youth's pride, and the painter, among men
At bay, where never pencil comes nor pen,
And shut about with his own frozen breath.
To others, for whom only rhyme wins faith
As poets,—only paint as painters,—then
He turns in the cold silence; and again
Shrinking, 'I am not as these are,' he saith.

And say that this is so, what follows it?
For were thine eyes set backwards in thine head,
Such words were well; but they see on, and far.
Unto the lights of the great Past, new-lit
Fair for the Future's track, look thou instead,—
Say thou instead 'I am not as *these* are.'

III. THE HUSBANDMEN

Though God, as one that is an householder,
Called these to labour in his vine-yard first,
Before the husk of darkness was well burst
Bidding them grope their way out and bestir,
(Who, questioned of their wages, answered, 'Sir,
Unto each man a penny:') though the worst
Burthen of heat was theirs and the dry thirst:
Though God hath since found none such as these were

To do their work like them:—Because of this
Stand not ye idle in the market-place.
Which of ye knoweth *he* is not that last
Who may be first by faith and will?—yea, his
The hand which after the appointed days
And hours shall give a Future to their Past?

SOUL'S BEAUTY

Under the arch of Life, where love and death,
Terror and mystery, guard her shrine, I saw
Beauty enthroned; and though her gaze struck awe,
I drew it in as simply as my breath.
Hers are the eyes which, over and beneath,
The sky and sea bend on thee,—which can draw,
By sea or sky or woman, to one law,
The allotted bondman of her palm and wreath.

This is that Lady Beauty, in whose praise
Thy voice and hand shake still,—long known to thee
By flying hair and fluttering hem,—the beat
Following her daily of thy heart and feet,
How passionately and irretrievably,
In what fond flight, how many ways and days!

BODY'S BEAUTY

Of Adam's first wife, Lilith, it is told
(The witch he loved before the gift of Eve,)
That, ere the snake's, her sweet tongue could deceive,
And her enchanted hair was the first gold.
And still she sits, young while the earth is old,
And, subtly of herself contemplative,
Draws men to watch the bright web she can weave,
Till heart and body and life are in its hold.

The rose and poppy are her flowers; for where
Is he not found, 0 Lilith, whom shed scent
And soft-shed kisses and soft sleep shall snare?
Lo! as that youth's eyes burned at thine, so went
Thy spell through him, and left his straight neck bent
And round his heart one strangling golden hair.

THE MONOCHORD

Is it this sky's vast vault or ocean's sound
That is Life's self and draws my life from me,
And by instinct ineffable decree
Holds my breath quailing on the bitter bound?
Nay, is it Life or Death, thus thunder-crown'd,
That 'mid the tide of all emergency
Now notes my separate wave, and to what sea
Its difficult eddies labour in the ground?

Oh! what is this that knows the road I came,
The flame turned cloud, the cloud returned to flame,
The lifted shifted steeps and all the way?—
That draws round me at last this wind-warm space,
And in regenerate rapture turns my face
Upon the devious coverts of dismay?

FROM DAWN TO NOON

As the child knows not if his mother's face
Be fair; nor of his elders yet can deem
What each most is; but as of hill or stream
At dawn, all glimmering life surrounds his place:
Who yet, tow'rd noon of his half-weary race,
Pausing awhile beneath the high sun-beam
And gazing steadily back,—as through a dream,
In things long past new features now can trace:—

Even so the thought that is at length fullgrown
Turns back to note the sun-smit paths, all grey
And marvellous once, where first it walked alone;
And haply doubts, amid the unblenching day,
Which most or least impelled its onward way,—
Those unknown things or these things overknown.

MEMORIAL THRESHOLDS

What place so strange,—though unrevealed snow
With unimaginable fires arise
At the earth's end,—what passion of surprise
Like frost-bound fire-girt scenes of long ago?
Lo! this is none but I this hour; and lo!
This is the very place which to mine eyes
Those mortal hours in vain immortalize,
'Mid hurrying crowds, with what alone I know.

City, of thine a single simple door,
By some new Power reduplicate, must be
Even yet my life-porch in eternity,
Even with one presence filled, as once of yore
Or mocking winds whirl round a chaff-strown floor
Thee and thy years and these my words and me.

HOARDED JOY

I said: 'Nay, pluck not,—let the first fruit be:
Even as thou sayest, it is sweet and red,
But let it ripen still. The tree's bent head
Sees in the stream its own fecundity
And bides the day of fulness. Shall not we
At the sun's hour that day possess the shade,

And claim our fruit before its ripeness fade,
And eat it from the branch and praise the tree?'

I say: 'Alas! our fruit hath wooed the sun
Too long,—'tis fallen and floats adown the stream.
Lo, the last clusters! Pluck them every one,
And let us sup with summer; ere the gleam
Of autumn set the year's pent sorrow free,
And the woods wail like echoes from the sea.'

BARREN SPRING

So now the changed year's turning wheel returns
And as a girl sails balanced in the wind,
And now before and now again behind
Stoops as it swoops, with cheek that laughs and burns,—
So Spring comes merry towards me now, but earns
No answering smile from me, whose life is twin'd
With the dead boughs that winter still must bind,
And whom to-day the Spring no more concerns.

Behold, this crocus is a withering flame;
This snowdrop, snow; this apple-blossom's part
To breed the fruit that breeds the serpent's art.
Nay, for these Spring-flowers, turn thy face from them,
Nor gaze till on the year's last lily-stem
The white cup shrivels round the golden heart.

FAREWELL TO THE GLEN

Sweet stream-fed glen, why say 'farewell' to thee
Who far'st so well and find'st for ever smooth
The brow of Time where man may read no ruth?
Nay, do thou rather say 'farewell' to me,
Who now fare forth in bitterer fantasy
Than erst was mine where other shade might soothe
By other streams, what while in fragrant youth
The bliss of being sad made melancholy.

And yet, farewell! For better shalt thou fare
When children bathe sweet faces in thy flow
And happy lovers blend sweet shadows there
In hours to come, than when an hour ago
Thine echoes had but one man's sighs to bear
And thy trees whispered what he feared to know.

VAIN VIRTUES

What is the sorriest thing that enters Hell?
None of the sins,—but this and that fair deed
Which a soul's sin at length could supersede.
These yet are virgins, whom death's timely knell
Might once have sainted; whom the fiends compel
Together now, in snake-bound shuddering sheaves
Of anguish, while the scorching bridegroom leaves
Their refuse maidenhood abominable.

Night sucks them down, the garbage of the pit,
Whose names, half entered in the book of Life,
Were God's desire at noon. And as their hair
And eyes sink last, the Torturer deigns no whit
To gaze, but, yearning, waits his worthier wife,
The Sin still blithe on earth that sent them there.

LOST DAYS

The lost days of my life until to-day,
What were they, could I see them on the street
Lie as they fell? Would they be ears of wheat
Sown once for food but trodden into clay?
Or golden coins squandered and still to pay?
Or drops of blood dabbling the guilty feet?
Or such spilt water as in dreams must cheat
The throats of men in Hell, who thirst alway?

I do not see them here; but after death
God knows I know the faces I shall see,
Each one a murdered self, with low last breath.
'I am thyself, — what hast thou done to me?'
'And I—and I—thyself,' (lo! each one saith,)
'And thou thyself to all eternity!'

DEATH'S SONGSTERS

When first that horse, within whose populous womb
The birth was death, o'ershadowed Troy with fate,
Her elders, dubious of its Grecian freight,
Brought Helen there to sing the songs of home:
She whispered, 'Friends, I am alone; come, come!'
Then, crouched within, Ulysses waxed afraid,
And on his comrades' quivering mouths he laid
His hands, and held them till the voice was dumb.

The same was he who, lashed to his own mast,
There where the sea-flowers screen the charnel-caves,
Beside the sirens' singing island pass'd,
Till sweetness failed along the inveterate waves...
Say, soul,—are songs of Death no heaven to thee,
Nor shames her lip the cheek of Victory?

HERO'S LAMP

That lamp thou fill'st in Eros name to-night,
0 Hero, shall the Sestian augurs take
To-morrow, and for drowned Leander's sake
To Anteros its fireless lip shall plight.
Aye, waft the unspoken vow: yet dawn's first light
On ebbing storm and life twice ebb'd must break;

While 'neath no sunrise, by the Avernian Lake,
Lo where Love walks, Death's pallid neophyte.

That lamp within Anteros' shadowy shrine
Shall stand unlit (for so the gods decree)
Till some one man the happy issue see
Of a life's love, and bid its flame to shine:
Which still may rest unfir'd; for, theirs or thine,
0 brother, what brought love to them or thee?

After the deaths of Leander and Hero, the signal-lamp was dedicated to Anteros, witIl the edict that no man should light it unless his love had proved fortunate.

THE TREES OF THE GARDEN

Ye who have passed Death's haggard hills; and ye
Whom trees that knew your sires shall cease to know
And still stand silent:—is it all a show,
A wisp that laughs upon the wall?—decree
Of some inexorable supremacy
Which ever, as man strains his blind surmise
From depth to ominous depth, looks past his eyes,
Sphinx-faced with unabashed augury?

Nay, rather question the Earth's self. Invoke
The storm-felled forest-trees moss-grown to-day
Whose roots are hillocks where the children play;
Or ask the silver sapling 'neath what yoke
Those stars, his spray-crown's clustering gems, shall wage
Their journey still when his boughs shrink with age.'

RETRO ME, SATHANA!'

Get thee behind me. Even as, heavy-curled,
Stooping against the wind, a charioteer
Is snatched from out his chariot by the hair,
So shall Time be; and as the void car, hurled
Abroad by reinless steeds, even so the world:
Yea, even as chariot-dust upon the air,
It shall be sought and not found anywhere.
Get thee behind me, Satan. Oft unfurled,
Thy perilous wings can beat and break like lath
Much mightiness of men to win thee praise.
Leave these weak feet to tread in narrow ways.
Thou still, upon the broad vine-sheltered path,
Mayst wait the turning of the phials of wrath
For certain years, for certain months and days.

LOST ON BOTH SIDES

As when two men have loved a woman well,
Each hating each, through Love's and Death's deceit;
Since not for either this stark marriage-sheet
And the long pauses of this wedding bell;
Yet o'er her grave the night and day dispel
At last their feud forlorn, with cold and heat;
Nor other than dear friends to death may fleet
The two lives left that most of her can tell:—

So separate hopes, which in a soul had wooed
The one same Peace, strove with each other long,
And Peace before their faces perished since:
So through that soul, in restless brotherhood,
They roam together now, and wind among
Its bye-streets, knocking at the dusty inns.

THE SUN'S SHAME

I

Beholding youth and hope in mockery caught
From life; and mocking pulses that remain
When the soul's death of bodily death is fain;
Honour unknown, and honour known unsought;
And penury's sedulous self-torturing thought
On gold, whose master therewith buys his bane;
And longed-for woman longing all in vain
For lonely man with love's desire distraught;
And wealth, and strength, and power, and pleasantness,
Given unto bodies of whose souls men say,
None poor and weak, slavish and foul, as they:—
Beholding these things, I behold no less
The blushing morn and blushing eve confess
The shame that loads the intolerable day.As some true chief of men, bowed down with stress
Of life's disastrous eld, on blossoming youth
May gaze, and murmur with self-pity and ruth,
'Might I thy fruitless treasure but possess,

Such blessing of mine all coming years should bless;'—
Then sends one sigh forth to the unknown goal,
And bitterly feels breathe against his soul
The hour swift-winged of nearer nothingness:—

Even so the World's grey Soul to the green World
Perchance one hour must cry: 'Woe's me, for whom
Inveteracy of ill portends the doom,—
Whose heart's old fire in shadow of shame is furl'd:
While thou even as of yore art journeying,
All soulless now, yet merry with the Spring!'

MICHELANGELO'S KISS

Great Michelangelo, with age grown bleak
And uttermost labours, having once o'ersaid
All grievous memories on his long life shed,
This worst regret to one true heart could speak:—
That when, with sorrowing love and reverence meek,
He stooped o'er sweet Colonna's dying bed,
His Muse and dominant Lady, spirit-wed,
Her hand he kissed, but not her brow or cheek.

0 Buonarruoti,—good at Art's fire-wheels
To urge her chariot!—even thus the Soul,
Touching at length some sorely-chastened goal,
Earns oftenest but a little: her appeals
Were deep and mute,—lowly her claim. Let be:
What holds for her Death's garner? And for thee?

THE VASE OF LIFE

Around the vase of Life at your slow pace
He has not crept, but turned it with his hands,
And all its sides already understands.
There, girt, one breathes alert for some great race;
Whose road runs far by sands and fruitful space;
Who laughs, yet through the jolly throng has pass'd;
Who weeps, nor stays for weeping; who at last,
A youth, stands somewhere crowned, with silent face.

And he has filled this vase with wine for blood,
With blood for tears, with spice for burning vow,
With watered flowers for buried love most fit;
And would have cast it shattered to the flood,
Yet in Fate's name has kept it whole; which now
Stands empty till his ashes fall in it.

LIFE THE BELOVED

As thy friend's face, with shadow of soul o'erspread,
Somewhile unto thy sight perchance hath been
Ghastly and strange, yet never so is seen
In thought, but to all fortunate favour wed;
As thy love's death-bound features never dead
To memory's glass return, but contravene

Frail fugitive days, and always keep, I ween
Than all new life a livelier lovelihead:—

So Life herself, thy spirit's friend and love,
Even still as Spring's authentic harbinger
Glows with fresh hours for hope to glorify;
Though pale she lay when in the winter grove
Her funeral flowers were snow-flakes shed on her
And the red wings of frost-fire rent the sky.

A SUPERSCRIPTION

Look in my face; my name is Might-have-been;
I am also called No-more, Too-late, Farewell;
Unto thine ear I hold the dead-sea shell
Cast up thy Life's foam-fretted feet between;
Unto thine eyes the glass where that is seen
Which had Life's form and Love's, but by my spell
Is now a shaken shadow intolerable,
Of ultimate things unuttered the frail screen.

Mark me, how still I am! But should there dart
One moment through thy soul the soft surprise
Of that winged Peace which lulls the breath of sighs,
Then shalt thou see me smile, and turn apart
Thy visage to mine ambush at thy heart
Sleepless with cold commemorative eyes.

HE AND I

Whence came his feet into my field, and why?
How is it that he sees it all so drear?
How do I see his seeing, and how hear
The name his bitter silence knows it by?
This was the little fold of separate sky
Whose pasturing clouds in the soul's atmosphere
Drew living light from one continual year:
How should he find it lifeless? He, or I?

Lo! this new Self now wanders round my field,
With plaints for every flower, and for each tree
A moan, the sighing wind's auxiliary:
And o'er sweet waters of my life, that yield
Unto his lips no draught but tears unseal'd,
Even in my place he weeps. Even I, not he.

NEWBORN DEATH

I

To-day Death seems to me an infant child
Which her worn mother Life upon my knee
Has set to grow my friend and play with me;
If haply so my heart might be beguil'd
To find no terrors in a face so mild,—

If haply so my weary heart might be
Unto the newborn milky eyes of thee,
O Death, before resentment reconcil'd.

How long, O Death? And shall thy feet depart
Still a young child's with mine, or wilt thou stand
Fullgrown the helpful daughter of my heart,
What time with thee indeed I reach the strand
Of the pale wave which knows thee what thou art,
And drink it in the hollow of thy hand?

II

And thou, O Life, the lady of all bliss,
With whom, when our first heart beat full and fast,
I wandered till the haunts of men were pass'd,
And in fair places found all bowers amiss
Till only woods and waves might hear our kiss,
While to the winds all thought of Death we cast:
Ah, Life! and must I have from thee at last
No smile to greet me and no babe but this?

Lo! Love, the child once ours; and Song, whose hair
Blew like a flame and blossomed like a wreath;
And Art, whose eyes were worlds by God found fair;
These o'er the book of Nature mixed their breath
With neck-twined arms, as oft we watched them there:
And did these die that thou mightst bear me Death?

THE ONE HOPE

When all desire at last and all regret
Go hand in hand to death, and all is vain,
What shall assuage the unforgotten pain
And teach the unforgetful to forget?
Shall Peace be still a sunk stream long unmet,—
Or may the soul at once in a green plain
Stoop through the spray of some sweet life-fountain
And cull the dew-drenched flowering amulet?

Ah! when the wan soul in that golden air
Between the scriptured petals softly blown
Peers breathless for the gift of grace unknown,
Ah! let none other written spell soe'er
But only the one Hope's one name be there,—
Not less nor more, but even that word alone.

www.bookjungle.com *email: sales@bookjungle.com fax: 630-214-0564 mail: Book Jungle PO Box 2226 Champaign, IL 61825*

The Codes Of Hammurabi And Moses
W. W. Davies

QTY

The discovery of the Hammurabi Code is one of the greatest achievements of archaeology, and is of paramount interest, not only to the student of the Bible, but also to all those interested in ancient history...

Religion **ISBN:** *1-59462-338-4* **Pages:132**
MSRP $12.95

The Theory of Moral Sentiments
Adam Smith

QTY

This work from 1749. contains original theories of conscience amd moral judgment and it is the foundation for systemof morals.

Philosophy **ISBN:** *1-59462-777-0* **Pages:536**
MSRP $19.95

Jessica's First Prayer
Hesba Stretton

QTY

In a screened and secluded corner of one of the many railway-bridges which span the streets of London there could be seen a few years ago, from five o'clock every morning until half past eight, a tidily set-out coffee-stall, consisting of a trestle and board, upon which stood two large tin cans, with a small fire of charcoal burning under each so as to keep the coffee boiling during the early hours of the morning when the work-people were thronging into the city on their way to their daily toil...

Pages:84

Childrens **ISBN:** *1-59462-373-2* *MSRP $9.95*

My Life and Work
Henry Ford

QTY

Henry Ford revolutionized the world with his implementation of mass production for the Model T automobile. Gain valuable business insight into his life and work with his own auto-biography... "We have only started on our development of our country we have not as yet, with all our talk of wonderful progress, done more than scratch the surface. The progress has been wonderful enough but..."

Pages:300

Biographies/ **ISBN:** *1-59462-198-5* *MSRP $21.95*

www.bookjungle.com email: sales@bookjungle.com fax: 630-214-0564 mail: Book Jungle PO Box 2226 Champaign, IL 61825

The Art of Cross-Examination
Francis Wellman

QTY

I presume it is the experience of every author, after his first book is published upon an important subject, to be almost overwhelmed with a wealth of ideas and illustrations which could readily have been included in his book, and which to his own mind, at least, seem to make a second edition inevitable. Such certainly was the case with me; and when the first edition had reached its sixth impression in five months, I rejoiced to learn that it seemed to my publishers that the book had met with a sufficiently favorable reception to justify a second and considerably enlarged edition. ...

Reference   ISBN: *1-59462-647-2*

Pages: 412
MSRP $19.95

On the Duty of Civil Disobedience
Henry David Thoreau

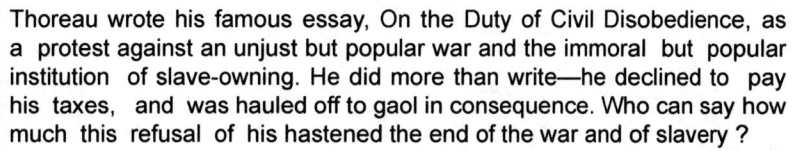

QTY

Thoreau wrote his famous essay, On the Duty of Civil Disobedience, as a protest against an unjust but popular war and the immoral but popular institution of slave-owning. He did more than write—he declined to pay his taxes, and was hauled off to gaol in consequence. Who can say how much this refusal of his hastened the end of the war and of slavery ?

Law   ISBN: *1-59462-747-9*

Pages: 48
MSRP $7.45

Dream Psychology Psychoanalysis for Beginners
Sigmund Freud

QTY

Sigmund Freud, born Sigismund Schlomo Freud (May 6, 1856 - September 23, 1939), was a Jewish-Austrian neurologist and psychiatrist who co-founded the psychoanalytic school of psychology. Freud is best known for his theories of the unconscious mind, especially involving the mechanism of repression; his redefinition of sexual desire as mobile and directed towards a wide variety of objects; and his therapeutic techniques, especially his understanding of transference in the therapeutic relationship and the presumed value of dreams as sources of insight into unconscious desires.

Psychology   ISBN: *1-59462-905-6*

Pages: 196
MSRP $15.45

The Miracle of Right Thought
Orison Swett Marden

QTY

Believe with all of your heart that you will do what you were made to do. When the mind has once formed the habit of holding cheerful, happy, prosperous pictures, it will not be easy to form the opposite habit. It does not matter how improbable or how far away this realization may see, or how dark the prospects may be, if we visualize them as best we can, as vividly as possible, hold tenaciously to them and vigorously struggle to attain them, they will gradually become actualized, realized in the life. But a desire, a longing without endeavor, a yearning abandoned or held indifferently will vanish without realization.

Self Help   ISBN: *1-59462-644-8*

Pages: 360
MSRP $25.45

www.bookjungle.com *email: sales@bookjungle.com fax: 630-214-0564 mail: Book Jungle PO Box 2226 Champaign, IL 61825*

QTY

- [ ] **The Rosicrucian Cosmo-Conception Mystic Christianity** by **Max Heindel** ISBN: *1-59462-188-8* **$38.95**
  The Rosicrucian Cosmo-conception is not dogmatic, neither does it appeal to any other authority than the reason of the student. It is: not controversial, but is: sent forth in the, hope that it may help to clear.. New Age/Religion Pages 646

- [ ] **Abandonment To Divine Providence** by **Jean-Pierre de Caussade** ISBN: *1-59462-228-0* **$25.95**
  "The Rev. Jean Pierre de Caussade was one of the most remarkable spiritual writers of the Society of Jesus in France in the 18th Century. His death took place at Toulouse in 1751. His works have gone through many editions and have been republished..." Inspirational/Religion Pages 400

- [ ] **Mental Chemistry** by **Charles Haanel** ISBN: *1-59462-192-6* **$23.95**
  Mental Chemistry allows the change of material conditions by combining and appropriately utilizing the power of the mind. Much like applied chemistry creates something new and unique out of careful combinations of chemicals the mastery of mental chemistry... New Age Pages 354

- [ ] **The Letters of Robert Browning and Elizabeth Barret Barrett 1845-1846 vol II** ISBN: *1-59462-193-4* **$35.95**
  by **Robert Browning** and **Elizabeth Barrett** Biographies Pages 596

- [ ] **Gleanings In Genesis (volume I)** by **Arthur W. Pink** ISBN: *1-59462-130-6* **$27.45**
  Appropriately has Genesis been termed "the seed plot of the Bible" for in it we have, in germ form, almost all of the great doctrines which are afterwards fully developed in the books of Scripture which follow... Religion/Inspirational Pages 420

- [ ] **The Master Key** by **L. W. de Laurence** ISBN: *1-59462-001-6* **$30.95**
  In no branch of human knowledge has there been a more lively increase of the spirit of research during the past few years than in the study of Psychology, Concentration and Mental Discipline. The requests for authentic lessons in Thought Control, Mental Discipline and... New Age/Business Pages 422

- [ ] **The Lesser Key Of Solomon Goetia** by **L. W. de Laurence** ISBN: *1-59462-092-X* **$9.95**
  This translation of the first book of the "Lernegton" which is now for the first time made accessible to students of Talismanic Magic was done, after careful collation and edition, from numerous Ancient Manuscripts in Hebrew, Latin, and French... New Age/Occult Pages 92

- [ ] **Rubaiyat Of Omar Khayyam** by **Edward Fitzgerald** ISBN: *1-59462-332-5* **$13.95**
  Edward Fitzgerald, whom the world has already learned, in spite of his own efforts to remain within the shadow of anonymity, to look upon as one of the rarest poets of the century, was born at Bredfield, in Suffolk, on the 31st of March, 1809. He was the third son of John Purcell... Music Pages 172

- [ ] **Ancient Law** by **Henry Maine** ISBN: *1-59462-128-4* **$29.95**
  The chief object of the following pages is to indicate some of the earliest ideas of mankind, as they are reflected in Ancient Law, and to point out the relation of those ideas to modern thought. Religion/History Pages 452

- [ ] **Far-Away Stories** by **William J. Locke** ISBN: *1-59462-129-2* **$19.45**
  "Good wine needs no bush, but a collection of mixed vintages does. And this book is just such a collection. Some of the stories I do not want to remain buried for ever in the museum files of dead magazine-numbers an author's not unpardonable vanity..." Fiction Pages 272

- [ ] **Life of David Crockett** by **David Crockett** ISBN: *1-59462-250-7* **$27.45**
  "Colonel David Crockett was one of the most remarkable men of the times in which he lived. Born in humble life, but gifted with a strong will, an indomitable courage, and unremitting perseverance... Biographies/New Age Pages 424

- [ ] **Lip-Reading** by **Edward Nitchie** ISBN: *1-59462-206-X* **$25.95**
  Edward B. Nitchie, founder of the New York School for the Hard of Hearing, now the Nitchie School of Lip-Reading, Inc, wrote "LIP-READING Principles and Practice". The development and perfecting of this meritorious work on lip-reading was an undertaking... How-to Pages 400

- [ ] **A Handbook of Suggestive Therapeutics, Applied Hypnotism, Psychic Science** ISBN: *1-59462-214-0* **$24.95**
  by **Henry Munro** Health/New Age/Health/Self-help Pages 376

- [ ] **A Doll's House: and Two Other Plays** by **Henrik Ibsen** ISBN: *1-59462-112-8* **$19.95**
  Henrik Ibsen created this classic when in revolutionary 1848 Rome. Introducing some striking concepts in playwriting for the realist genre, this play has been studied the world over. Fiction/Classics/Plays 308

- [ ] **The Light of Asia** by **sir Edwin Arnold** ISBN: *1-59462-204-3* **$13.95**
  In this poetic masterpiece, Edwin Arnold describes the life and teachings of Buddha. The man who was to become known as Buddha to the world was born as Prince Gautama of India but he reached the worldly riches and abandoned the reigns of power when... Religion/History/Biographies Pages 170

- [ ] **The Complete Works of Guy de Maupassant** by **Guy de Maupassant** ISBN: *1-59462-157-8* **$16.95**
  "For days and days, nights and nights, I had dreamed of that first kiss which was to consecrate our engagement, and I knew not on what spot I should put my lips..." Fiction/Classics Pages 240

- [ ] **The Art of Cross-Examination** by **Francis L. Wellman** ISBN: *1-59462-309-0* **$26.95**
  Written by a renowned trial lawyer, Wellman imparts his experience and uses case studies to explain how to use psychology to extract desired information through questioning. How-to/Science/Reference Pages 408

- [ ] **Answered or Unanswered?** by **Louisa Vaughan** ISBN: *1-59462-248-5* **$10.95**
  Miracles of Faith in China Religion Pages 112

- [ ] **The Edinburgh Lectures on Mental Science (1909)** by **Thomas** ISBN: *1-59462-008-3* **$11.95**
  This book contains the substance of a course of lectures recently given by the writer in the Queen Street Hall, Edinburgh. Its purpose is to indicate the Natural Principles governing the relation between Mental Action and Material Conditions... New Age/Psychology Pages 148

- [ ] **Ayesha** by **H. Rider Haggard** ISBN: *1-59462-301-5* **$24.95**
  Verily and indeed it is the unexpected that happens! Probably if there was one person upon the earth from whom the Editor of this, and of a certain previous history, did not expect to hear again... Classics Pages 380

- [ ] **Ayala's Angel** by **Anthony Trollope** ISBN: *1-59462-352-X* **$29.95**
  The two girls were both pretty, but Lucy who was twenty-one who supposed to be simple and comparatively unattractive, whereas Ayala was credited, as her Bombwhat romantic name might show, with poetic charm and a taste for romance. Ayala when her father died was nineteen... Fiction Pages 484

- [ ] **The American Commonwealth** by **James Bryce** ISBN: *1-59462-286-8* **$34.45**
  An interpretation of American democratic political theory. It examines political mechanics and society from the perspective of Scotsman James Bryce Politics Pages 572

- [ ] **Stories of the Pilgrims** by **Margaret P. Pumphrey** ISBN: *1-59462-116-0* **$17.95**
  This book explores pilgrims religious oppression in England as well as their escape to Holland and eventual crossing to America on the Mayflower, and their early days in New England... History Pages 268

www.bookjungle.com *email:* sales@bookjungle.com *fax:* 630-214-0564 *mail:* Book Jungle PO Box 2226 Champaign, IL 61825

QTY

The Fasting Cure *by Sinclair Upton*   ISBN: *1-59462-222-1*   **$13.95**
In the Cosmopolitan Magazine for May, 1910, and in the Contemporary Review (London) for April, 1910, I published an article dealing with my experiences in fasting. I have written a great many magazine articles, but never one which attracted so much attention... *New Age/Self Help/Health Pages 164*

Hebrew Astrology *by Sepharial*   ISBN: *1-59462-308-2*   **$13.45**
In these days of advanced thinking it is a matter of common observation that we have left many of the old landmarks behind and that we are now pressing forward to greater heights and to a wider horizon than that which represented the mind-content of our progenitors... *Astrology Pages 144*

Thought Vibration or The Law of Attraction in the Thought World   ISBN: *1-59462-127-6*   **$12.95**
by William Walker Atkinson   *Psychology/Religion Pages 144*

Optimism *by Helen Keller*   ISBN: *1-59462-108-X*   **$15.95**
Helen Keller was blind, deaf, and mute since 19 months old, yet famously learned how to overcome these handicaps, communicate with the world, and spread her lectures promoting optimism. An inspiring read for everyone... *Biographies/Inspirational Pages 84*

Sara Crewe *by Frances Burnett*   ISBN: *1-59462-360-0*   **$9.45**
In the first place, Miss Minchin lived in London. Her home was a large, dull, tall one, in a large, dull square, where all the houses were alike, and all the sparrows were alike, and where all the door-knockers made the same heavy sound... *Childrens/Classic Pages 88*

The Autobiography of Benjamin Franklin *by Benjamin Franklin*   ISBN: *1-59462-135-7*   **$24.95**
The Autobiography of Benjamin Franklin has probably been more extensively read than any other American historical work, and no other book of its kind has had such ups and downs of fortune. Franklin lived for many years in England, where he was agent... *Biographies/History Pages 332*

Name	
Email	
Telephone	
Address	
City, State ZIP	

☐ Credit Card   ☐ Check / Money Order

Credit Card Number	
Expiration Date	
Signature	

Please Mail to: Book Jungle
PO Box 2226
Champaign, IL 61825
or Fax to: 630-214-0564

ORDERING INFORMATION

web: *www.bookjungle.com*
email: *sales@bookjungle.com*
fax: *630-214-0564*
mail: *Book Jungle PO Box 2226 Champaign, IL 61825*
or PayPal *to sales@bookjungle.com*

Please contact us for bulk discounts

DIRECT-ORDER TERMS

20% Discount if You Order Two or More Books
Free Domestic Shipping!
Accepted: Master Card, Visa, Discover, American Express

Lightning Source UK Ltd.
Milton Keynes UK
UKOW02f2031140214

226486UK00005B/259/P